Hola, DOMINICAN REPUBLIC

by Meghan Gottschall

CHERRY LAKE PUBLISHING • ANN ARBOR, MICHIGAN

Cherry Lake Press

Published in the United States of America by Cherry Lake Publishing Group
Ann Arbor, Michigan
www.cherrylakepublishing.com

Reading Adviser: Marla Conn, MS, Ed., Literacy specialist, Read-Ability, Inc.

Photo Credits: ©DigitalVision Vectors/jack0m/Getty Images, cover (globe); ©Danieloncarevic/iStock/Getty Images, cover (top); ©peeterv/iStock/Getty Images, cover (bottom); ©itsten/iStock Editorial/Getty Images, 1; ©ayzek/iStock/Getty Images, 3; ©Anna Smirnova/EyeEm/Getty Images, 4; ©Kit Korzun/fStop/Getty Images, 5; ©PeterHermesFurian/iStock/Getty Images, 6; ©Theocharis Leontarakis/EyeEm/Getty Images, 7; ©Isaac Ruiz Santana/iStock/Getty Images, 8; ©Das Nili/Wikimedia, 9; ©Rafael Morillo/EyeEm/Getty Images, 10; ©NASA/ Wikimedia, 11; ©frank wouters/Wikimedia, 12; ©Wiktor/Pixabay, 13; ©Spencer Platt/Getty Images, 14; ©darwin1809/Pixabay, 16; ©Svetlana-Cherruty/iStock/Getty Images, 17 (coffee); ©cgdeaw/iStock/Getty Images, 17 (sugarcane); ©Borisenkov Andrei/iStock/Getty Images, 17 (sugar); ©Nino_sayompoo/iStock/Getty Images, 17 (dishes); ©José Grullón/Wikimedia, 18; ©EFE/Orlando Barria/Newscom, 19; ©Presidencia El Salvador/Wikimedia, 20; ©Harry Benson/Hulton Archive/Getty Images, 21; ©Walter Bibikow/Digital Vision/Getty Images, 22; ©Oscar Montilla/Moment/Getty Images, 23; ©JudyDillon/iStock Editorial/Getty Images, 24; ©czekma13/iStock Editorial/Getty Images, 25; ©Aleksandr Rybalko/iStock/Getty Images, 26; ©Aleksandr Rybalko/iStock/Getty Images, 27 (middle); ©Aleksandr Rybalko/iStock/Getty Images, 27 (bottom); ©Marvin del Cid/Moment Open/Getty Images, 27 (top); ©Mike Ehrmann/Getty Images, 28; ©Mike Ehrmann/Getty Images, 29; ©Mariordo/Wikimedia, 30; ©Anatoly Kireev/iStock Editorial/Getty Images, 31; ©Mario De Moya F/iStock Editorial/Getty Images, 32; ©Mario De Moya F/iStock Editorial/Getty Images, 33; ©Nirad/iStock/Getty Images, 34; ©Mario De Moya F/iStock Editorial/Getty Images, 35; ©Xinhua News Agency/Fran Afonso/Newscom, 36; ©Eloy Rodriguez/Moment Unreleased/Getty Images, 38; ©rchphoto/iStock Editorial/Getty Images, 39; ©Luciano Ippolito/iStock/Getty Images, 40; ©Mariâ Kalinina/EyeEm/Getty Images, 41; ©ukayacan/iStock Unreleased/Getty Images, 42 (bottom); ©atlantic-kid/iStock Editorial/Getty Images, 42 (top); ©EPKIN/iStock/Getty Images, 43; ©Jane Sweeney/Alloy/Getty Images, 44; ©ALLEKO/iStock/Getty Images, 45; ©DigitalVision Vectors/filo/Getty Images, background

Cherry Lake Press is an imprint of Cherry Lake Publishing Group.

Library of Congress Cataloging-in-Publication Data has been filed and is available at catalog.loc.gov

Cherry Lake Publishing Group would like to acknowledge the work of the Partnership for 21st Century Learning, a Network of Battelle for Kids. Please visit http://www.battelleforkids.org/networks/p21 for more information.

Printed in the United States of America
Corporate Graphics

TABLE OF CONTENTS

CHAPTER 1
Welcome to the Dominican Republic! 4

CHAPTER 2
**Business and Government
in the Dominican Republic** 13

CHAPTER 3
Meet the People 22

CHAPTER 4
Celebrations 30

CHAPTER 5
What's for Dinner? 38

Glossary 46

For More Information 47

Index 48

About the Author 48

WELCOME TO THE DOMINICAN REPUBLIC!

The Dominican coastline has around 800 miles (1,288 kilometers) of beaches.

The Dominican Republic is a country in the Caribbean. It is on the island of Hispaniola. This is the second-largest island in the region, after Cuba. The nation takes up the eastern two-thirds of the land. Haiti is on the western side. This country is the Dominican Republic's only neighbor. The Caribbean Sea and the North Atlantic Ocean form its water borders. Puerto Rico is about 80 miles (129 km) to the east.

The country's area is approximately 18,653 square miles (48,311 square km). This is about twice the size of New Hampshire. Around 11 million people live there.

Spanish, African, and Amerindian cultures have all influenced life in the Dominican Republic. The country's food, festivals, and religious customs reflect its rich history.

Humpback Whales, Samaná Bay

From December to March every year, thousands of humpback whales migrate to the Samaná Bay. There they mate and give birth. The whales then return to the colder waters of the North Atlantic Ocean. This behavior has existed for a long time. Cave paintings of whales were made by the first inhabitants of Hispaniola.

ACTIVITY

Take a close look at the map of the island of Hispaniola. Trace the borders of the Dominican Republic. Label Haiti, Santo Domingo, the Atlantic Ocean, and the Caribbean Sea. Look online to fill in your map. Find the country's highest mountain, Duarte Peak. Label its lowest point, Lake Enriquillo. What other interesting places can you find?

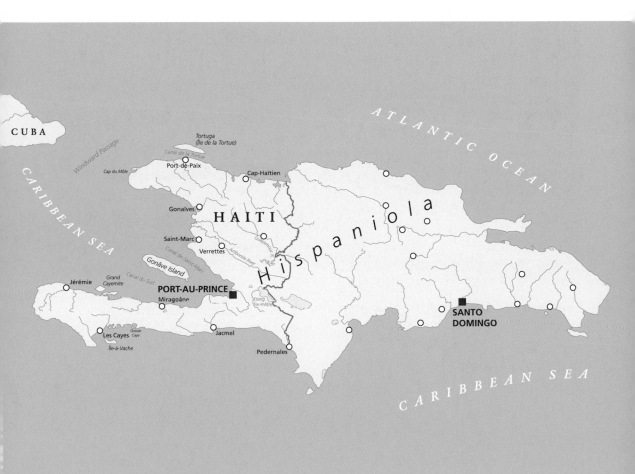

Brightly colored flamingos wade in the shallow water of the country's swamps and lakes.

The Dominican Republic contains a variety of ecosystems. There are major mountain ranges and **fertile** valleys. Low-lying plains give way to rainforests and pine forests. A **rift valley** and a large salt lake can also be found there.

The capital, Santo Domingo, is on the southern coast. The city is located in the coastal lowlands. These flat plains stretch east from Santo Domingo.

The Cordillera Central mountain range runs east to west across the center of the country. Duarte Peak is found there. At 10,417 feet (3,175 meters), it is the highest peak in the Caribbean.

Valle de Lilis is the final valley before Duarte Peak.

Taino Cave Paintings

The Cave of Wonders cave system is near the southern coast. The walls are covered in hundreds of Taino paintings. Some of these date to the 15th century. Scientists believe some may be thousands of years old. There are drawings of animals and human faces. Others are abstract. Their meaning is unknown today.

In the north, many crops grow in the fertile soil of the Cibao Valley. Santiago, the country's second-largest city, is in this region.

The western region near the border with Haiti is **arid**. Lake Enriquillo is a large salt lake found there. It is the lowest point in the entire Caribbean. The surface is 144 feet (44 m) below sea level.

The Dominican Republic is in a mild tropical zone. The average temperature is 82 degrees Fahrenheit (28 degrees Celsius) on the coast. In the mountains, the average is 69°F (21°C).

The northeast coast receives around 100 inches (2,540 millimeters) of rain a year. The west and southwest are much drier. In some parts, fewer than 30 inches (760 mm) of rain fall on average.

Dark clouds often bring brief rainstorms to the Dominican Republic on summer afternoons.

Hurricanes hit the Dominican Republic less often than other Caribbean nations. A major hurricane strikes the Dominican Republic about once every 20 years.

Tropical storms and hurricanes sometimes hit the island. High winds and rain cause damage and injury. They also create another problem. Garbage from the ocean and rivers is carried onto beaches during storms. In 2018, tropical storm Beryl dumped thousands of tons of garbage and plastic on Montesinos Beach, near Santo Domingo.

From storms to droughts, extreme weather causes many problems. Major droughts hit the island in 2018 and 2019. These have mostly affected the south, southwest, and northwest parts of the country. Lack of water has especially hurt cattle in these areas.

The Dominican Republic is home to many reptiles and amphibians. The spiny giant frog is critically **endangered**. Mining and agriculture are destroying its habitat. The Hispaniolan iguana is also endangered.

Pines and cedars grow in mountain areas. Palm trees and **mangroves** are tropical trees. More than 300 types of orchids can also be found on the island.

Solenodons

Solenodons are ancient mammals. They have existed for 76 million years. The animals used to be found all over North America. Today, they are only found on Cuba and Hispaniola. Solenodons are about a foot (30 cm) long. They look like shrews. Their sharp teeth can inject venom into prey.

CHAPTER 2

BUSINESS AND GOVERNMENT IN THE DOMINICAN REPUBLIC

The Dominican Republic has one of the fastest-growing economies in Latin America. Many people still live in poverty. The situation is improving.

Sugar, coffee, and tobacco were once the country's most important products. Today, the **tourism** industry is changing the economy. More than 6.5 million people visited in 2018. This is more than any other Caribbean country. New jobs in finance and construction are also helping.

Tourists visit seaside hotels to relax and enjoy the sun and water.

Poverty in the Dominican Republic

Around one-third of the Dominican population lives on less than $1.25 a day. **Rural** areas are affected by poverty the most. They do not benefit from tourism money.

The Dominican workforce has changed since the 1950s. Then, more than 70 percent of workers were employed in agriculture. Today, only 9 percent have these jobs. Around 71 percent of workers are in the service industry. These are mostly tourism jobs. People work in hotels, resorts, and restaurants. Industry jobs make up around 19 percent. This includes manufacturing and mining.

Crops like sugar, tobacco, coffee, and cacao have traditionally been the country's biggest exports. Today, gold is the biggest export. The mining industry also produces silver, nickel, and **bauxite**.

Agricultural products are still important exports. Citrus, vegetables, pineapples, and flowers are all sent to other countries.

The tourism industry has increased the need for different foods. Meat, chicken, cheese, and potatoes are recent imports.

2017 TRADING PARTNERS

The Dominican Republic has many important trading partners. It trades with countries all over the world. Trading partners are where a country sends its exports or where its imports come from. Here is a graph showing the Dominican Republic's top import and export trading partners.

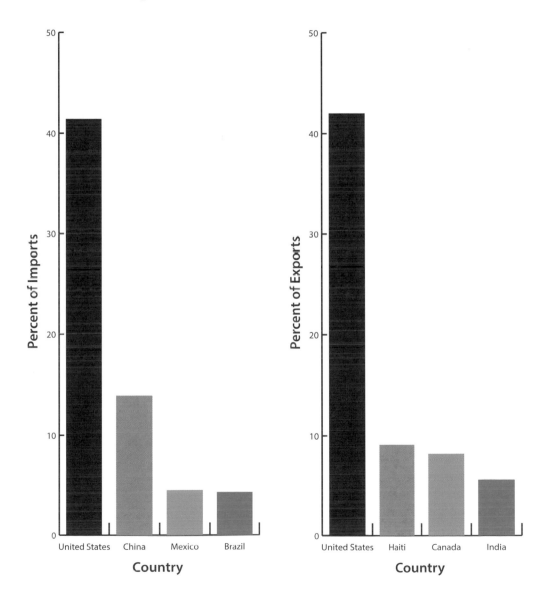

Many fruits and vegetables are grown in the Dominican Republic.

Agriculture has always been an important part of the Dominican economy. Around 50 percent of the land is currently used to grow crops and raise livestock. Farming is a risky industry. Hurricanes and tropical storms can destroy crops. Droughts are another problem. Other natural hazards like mudslides can also affect farms.

ACTIVITY

Pick a major Dominican export. You could pick sugar, coffee, or gold. Research its history and importance to the Dominican Republic. Make a timeline with five important dates.

What product did you choose? What has it contributed to the Dominican Republic's economy? Has its importance changed over the years?

Brown sugar and white sugar both come from pressed sugarcane stalks. Coffee comes from shrubs, and gold is mined from the ground.

For years, **dictators** were in charge of the Dominican Republic. Some of these were forceful military leaders called caudillos. People were afraid of them. The economy suffered. Many lived in poverty. The government was corrupt. It controlled the country's elections. Dictators wanted to keep their power.

The National Palace in Santo Domingo contains the offices of the executive branch.

Soy dominicano como tú

Soy dominicano y tengo derecho

Soy dominicano oy y tengo derecho

Soy domini...

Relationship with Haiti

Haiti and the Dominican Republic were once part of the same colony. Their relationship today is not an easy one. Many immigrants move from Haiti to the Dominican Republic. They are hoping to find better jobs. Many people oppose this. They say Dominicans won't be able to find work. The government sends many Haitian immigrants back to their home country. Even Dominicans of Haitian descent are sent back.

Since 1996, elections have generally been seen as less corrupt. The country is now a democratic republic. Presidents are elected to four-year terms. They can only be in power for two terms.

The president, vice president, and cabinet make up the executive branch. The legislative branch is made up of a senate and a chamber of deputies. At least 16 judges serve on the Supreme Court.

Citizens vote directly for the president. Members of the armed forces and the police are not allowed to vote in elections. This rule comes from the country's constitution.

In 2016, Danilo Medina Sánchez was reelected president. The country's election process had improved. There were still accusations of corruption. Medina's opponent accused him of using government money for his campaign. He said Medina had paid people not to vote. Violence broke out at the polls. Six people were killed.

President Medina is one of the founders of the Dominican Liberation Party (PLD).

U.S. Interventions

The United States has occupied the Dominican Republic several times. They took control from 1916 to 1924 when the economy started to decline. Thousands of U.S. Marines were stationed on the island. They occupied the country again from 1965 to 1966. The United States was afraid the country would turn to communism.

Medina is a member of the PLD. This has been the main party in power since 1996. Many people think a different group, called the Modern Revolutionary Party, will take charge after the 2020 elections.

The economy has been improving. Progress is still slow in some parts of the country. Life in rural areas and poor neighborhoods hasn't improved as much. Citizens are hoping a new president will help these areas.

CHAPTER 3

MEET THE PEOPLE

The Taino people were the first inhabitants of Hispaniola. In 1492, Christopher Columbus claimed the island for Spain. By 1697, the Spanish controlled the eastern side of the island. It was called Santo Domingo. The French were in charge of the western part that became Haiti.

Traditional Dominican clothing was influenced by European colonial style.

Many of the cities in the Dominican Republic boast very old colonial buildings.

Santo Domingo declared independence from Spain in 1821. Haitians then took over for 22 years. In 1844, the country gained independence again. It declared itself the Dominican Republic.

Today, more than 80 percent of the population lives in urban areas. Santo Domingo is the largest city, with a population of 2.5 million. Founded in 1496, it was the first permanent European town in the Americas. Santiago is the second-largest city. Its population is around 550,000. Around one in seven Dominicans lives outside of the country. It is estimated that more Dominicans live in New York City than in Santiago.

Most of the country's population are **descendants** of the island's Spanish **colonizers** and enslaved people from Africa. Around 70 percent identify as having mixed ancestry.

The brightly colored Creole dress is a famous part of Dominican culture. It was influenced by African styles and is worn for celebrations and feast days.

The official language of the Dominican Republic is Spanish. Words have been added from Arawak, the language of the Taino people. For example, "iguana" comes from an Arawak word that means "big lizard." Other words come from African languages.

Haitian Creole is a mix of French, Spanish, and West African languages. There are around 160,000 speakers in the Dominican Republic.

Samaná English has about 12,000 speakers. African American immigrants brought the language from the United States in 1824. Their descendants speak it today.

Children are required to go to school from around the ages of 6 to 14. This rule is not enforced, though. Around 40 percent of students drop out before the eighth grade.

Students used to attend school for 5 hours a day. Many had to work on farms to help their families. In 2014, the president made the school day 8 hours long. Students started to receive two free meals a day. The government is trying to improve the country's education levels.

All students in the Dominican Republic wear school uniforms.

ACTIVITY

TAINO ROCK PAINTINGS

Petroglyphs are carvings or drawings on rocks. The Taino people left behind many petroglyphs on Hispaniola. Some of these drawings represent the natural world. There are carvings of the sun, plants, and animals. Others represent the Taino gods.

MATERIALS

- Small rocks
- Permanent marker

INSTRUCTIONS

1. Research pictures of Taino cave paintings and rock carvings in this book and online. What do the pictures look like? What symbols did they use?

2. Using the marker, make your own rock paintings. Use the symbols you found as your guide.

Hoyo de Sanabe Cave contains one of the largest collections of Taino rock paintings.

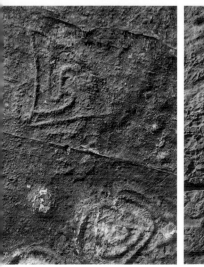

Baseball is the most popular sport in the Dominican Republic. Many children want to play professionally. Some teenagers attend training camps. They are hoping to make it big. This is seen as a way out of poverty. Professional players can help their families. Some students drop out of school so they can focus on baseball. It is difficult to make it on a professional team. Very few of those who try out for major league teams make it.

The national baseball team of the Dominican Republic won the 2013 World Baseball Classic tournament.

Baseball

Baseball was introduced to Hispaniola in the 1880s. The first professional league was established in 1890. More than 750 Dominicans have become Major League Baseball players. The only country with more is the United States. Some players include Robinson Canó, Sammy Sosa, Manny Ramírez, and David Ortiz. Juan Marichal, Pedro Martínez, and Vladimir Guerrero are Dominican players in the National Baseball Hall of Fame.

CHAPTER 4

CELEBRATIONS

Around 68 percent of the population identifies as Catholic. Some studies put this number higher than 90 percent. This reflects the Dominican Republic's history as a Spanish colony. Santo Domingo is home to the oldest church in the Americas. It was completed in 1541. The country's flag features a cross and a Bible.

Santa María la Menor is one of the most important Christian sites in the Caribbean.

Vodou shamans are part of the traditionally Catholic Carnival parades.

Some of the practices of Dominican Catholicism include elements of folk religions. Many people believe that the Catholic saints have special protective powers. They keep pictures of one or two saints in their homes. This belief was influenced by African religions.

Religions like Santería and Vodou originated in West Africa. Vodou came to the Dominican Republic with Haitian immigrants. Up to 23 percent of the population are Protestants.

Most Dominican holidays are religious. Christmas is a big celebration. Adults and children set off fireworks. Families do a secret gift exchange. They eat a large dinner together on Christmas Eve. Many towns host Christmas parades. People play drums and *güiras*, a type of percussion instrument.

Carnival is celebrated in February. This festival has Catholic origins. It is celebrated before Lent. It has also been influenced by African traditions.

During the monthlong festival, there are parades every Sunday. People wear elaborate masks and costumes. These celebrate the folklore of the Dominican Republic. *El Roba la Gallina*, or "the Chicken Thief," is a comical character.

Careteros are craftsmen who make special masks for Carnival. They use an old Spanish technique. The masks also have African influences.

The holiday ends the first Sunday in March. There is one final parade in Santo Domingo on this day. Awards are given out for the best costumes and performances.

Many Dominicans enjoy time off work and spend holidays with their families.

Dominican celebrations of Carnival are known for their colorful costumes and their musical and dance performances.

HOLIDAYS AND CELEBRATIONS

January 1 – **New Year's Day**

January 6 – **Epiphany**

January 21 – **Our Lady of Altagracia**

January 26 – **Duarte's Day**

February – **Carnival**

February 27 – **Independence Day**

May or June – **Corpus Christi**

August 16 – **Restoration Day**

September 24 – **Our Lady of Mercy Day**

November 6 – **Constitution Day**

December 25 – **Christmas**

December 31 – **New Year's Eve**

ACTIVITY

The town of Cotuí has a unique Carnival tradition. People use recycled materials to make costumes and masks. Many look like animals. One group makes masks out of banana leaves. Another uses only shredded paper. Make your own Carnival mask!

MATERIALS

- Recycled materials: paper, fabric, etc.
- Markers
- Scissors
- Paper plate
- Glue
- Straw or wooden stick

INSTRUCTIONS

1. Use this book and the internet to find inspiration for your mask. Will yours represent an animal or folklore character, or be an abstract design?

2. Look around your house or school for materials you could use for your mask. What paper or fabric can you find? Be creative and find unusual materials to decorate your mask.

3. Cut a paper plate in half to use as the base of your mask.

4. Cut eye and nose holes in the paper plate.

5. Decorate your mask with the markers and the materials you found.

6. Attach the straw or wooden stick to the back of the paper plate. Place it on the side so you can hold the mask to your face.

Carnival masks are large and colorful.

The Dominican Republic has two national holidays that celebrate independence. February 27 is Independence Day. It recognizes the country's freedom from Haiti. The holiday falls during Carnival. It is typically the biggest day of celebration during this festival.

Restoration Day is August 16. This holiday celebrates independence from Spain. Folk dancers perform in parades. They wear bright costumes. In election years, this is also the day that the new president takes over.

Music plays a huge part in Dominican festivals and celebrations. People dance and sing to celebrate. Dominican music mixes rhythms and instruments from different cultures.

The National Army band marches and plays in the Santo Domingo Independence Day parade.

Merengue is the national music of the Dominican Republic. The three main instruments used in merengue reflect the country's cultural history. The accordion is an instrument of Spanish origin. The *tambora* is an African drum. The *güira* is a Taino percussion instrument.

Bachata is another popular kind of music. This slow dance music started in rural areas of the country in the 1950s. Very popular in dance halls, modern bachata mixes Latin and African beats.

Music is not only used for entertainment. *Palo* is a form of religious music that originated in West Africa. Mixing drums and singing, it is performed by two or three drummers at religious ceremonies.

CHAPTER 5

WHAT'S FOR DINNER?

Food in the Dominican Republic has been influenced by the country's history. Spanish, African, and Taino elements can be found in many recipes. Dishes also feature local ingredients. Starches like rice, potatoes, and **cassava** all grow on the island. Bananas and **plantains** are popular.

Fruits and vegetables are commonly sold in outdoor markets.

Mangú is a dish of boiled and mashed plantains. People often eat it at breakfast. The dish has West African and Taino roots. *Locrio* is made of seasoned rice. It is often served with chicken or pork. This meal is similar to the Spanish rice dish paella. *Casabe* is a Taino flatbread made from cassava. It is commonly served with soups or stews.

Rice is the most common food in the Dominican Republic. The population eats around 50,000 tons of this food every month. Herbs like cilantro and thyme are used to flavor dishes. Other common seasonings are cumin, garlic, onion, and lime.

Carrot is used in many rice dishes and stews.

From March through June, lobsters cannot be caught or even served at restaurants in the Dominican Republic. This protects lobsters during their mating season.

Many meals include meat such as pork, beef, chicken, and goat. One method of preparing meat is by stewing it. This is called *guisado*. There is lots of access to seafood. Many people eat fish such as grouper or snapper. Octopus, crab, and lobster are also popular to eat.

Many tropical fruits are popular in the Dominican Republic. Some are not as common in the United States, such as mamey, star fruit, and guanabana.

Frying is a popular method of preparing Dominican dishes. Fish is often fried. *Pastelitos* are another fried food. They are similar to empanadas. Dough is filled with meat and vegetables. Tostones are fried green plantains. They are often served as a side dish.

Drinks are prepared with local tropical fruits. Passion fruit juice, papaya milkshakes, and coconut water and milk are all popular. Roadside stands serve local coffee.

There is a long tradition of fishing in the Dominican Republic.